MRS. JERNINGHAM'S JOURNAL.

NEW YORK:
CHARLES SCRIBNER & COMPANY.
1870.

MRS. JERNINGHAM'S JOURNAL.

PART I.

MARRIED six weary weeks to-day!
How sad is life that was so gay!
How desolate the street appears—
  Alas, that I must live in it!
I see the houses through my tears,
  And do not like the sight one bit!

How can I pass the heavy hours
Without my darling birds and flow'rs—
A scamper on the lawn—a ride—

With other girls a merry chatter,
Where we our partners can deride,
The merits of our dress decide,
And settle much important matter?

A comfortable luncheon, then
Croquet, or archery; and tea
With half a dozen lively men
Who come to laugh and flirt with *me?*

O life was sweet and beautiful!
Its pretty pleasures all my own;
O life of life was very full,
And ev'ry minute lived alone!

And ev'ry minute was so strong,
It brought its little new-born bliss,
Sweeping in tender light along,
Or leaving shadows like a kiss.

What lent its glory to the flow'r,
And gave the nightingale her pow'r,
And made the sky so very blue?
My little heart could it be you?

My little heart, why did you beat
  As if delighted to be me?
O, was it youth that was so sweet?
  Or was it youth's sweet liberty?

They said I danced when I should walk
  (My gay feet worked my gayer will);
They said I laughed when I should talk,
  And chattered when I should be still.

I'd wake with laughing in the night—
  Ah, happy nights I can't forget!—
I'd catch my dreams, they were so bright,
  And find my thoughts were brighter yet.

I'd wink my little eyes and peep,
 With slumber waging weary strife ;—
It seemed so hard to be asleep
 And lose the smallest bit of life!

Of life that moved with airy sway,
Like singing music—making play
Like wavelets dancing on the sea
In even measures—all for me!

And when the sun illumed the dark,
 I'd sing good morning to the sky,
And wake the little lazy lark,
 And curtsey to the butterfly.

O, sweet to flutter 'mid the grass,
 In charming dews the wise condemn,
And when the busy swallows pass
 To nod my friendly head at them!

It did the little squirrels good
  To see a thing as gay as I,
When I came running through the wood
  To hide from the delighted sky;

The quaint old cuckoo said his say,
  I mock'd him with my artful word;
I think he knows not to this day
  Whether I am a girl or bird!

'Twas 'cuckoo, cuckoo, cuckoo,' he;
  And 'cuckoo, cuckoo, cuckoo,' I;—
It was the grandest sight to see
  That puzzled cuckoo round me fly!

In ev'ry bird I found a friend—
  A confidante in ev'ry leaf;
The little breezes would attend,
  The robins knew I was their chief.

The good old trees would rustle so,
  In stately gossip, when I came;
The grass that kissed my feet, I know,
  Kissed no one else's quite the same.

Life was a most triumphant fact!—
  What could my ecstasy destroy?
I did not care to think or act—
  Just to be living was a joy!

O lovely earth! O lovely sky!—
I was in love with nature, I;
And nature was in love with me;—
O, lovely life—when I was free!

And then I'd spread my shining wings,
  And fly away without a care
To those bewitching balls and things
  Where I discovered I was fair.

And when I found how fair I am,
  I felt a new delight in life,
Nor guessed that Mr. Jerningham
  Had asked me from Papa as wife.

How vexed I was when I was told!
  I hardly could my patience keep;
And then Papa began to scold,
  And then poor I began to weep.

But one thing's pleasant, I confess;
  Marriage a trousseau doth entail;
I had to choose a satin dress,
  And was allowed to wear a veil!

The wedding day came all too soon—
  I'd rather it had not been mine—
But still I liked the Honeymoon
  At Paris and the pretty Rhine.

And now I've not a thing to do,
  And nobody to say a word;
I've got to keep my house, 'tis true,—
  I keep a house!—it's too absurd!

She's such a clever woman, Cook,
I heartily dislike her look;
She really seems to fancy I
Know nothing useful 'neath the sky,
And with her stuck-up chin and head
Her silence is a thing to dread!
And then when she begins to speak,
  She asks such dreadful questions—O!
How many quarts of milk a week
  Shall I require? how *should* I know!
And what may be the price of coals?
  How many tons will be enough?
Shall she take quartern loaves, or rolls?
  And do I want the kitchen stuff?

I've ordered dinner—'tis a fact
That I was frightened at the act!
Says I, 'A leg of lamb you'll get,'
Says she, 'It's not in season yet;'
So turning somewhere for relief,
I said, 'Then get a leg of beef:'
She look'd so keenly in my face
She made me feel the whole disgrace,
And so I cried, 'Get anything,'
And ran upstairs to play and sing:—
I hope we'll have *some* dinner, though,
Or John may be displeased, you know.

Why did they make me marry him?
Life *was* so bright and *is* so dim!
I cannot understand why men
Should stop their growth at five feet ten;
I meant my husband to be tall,—
    Short men have such a shabby look,—

And then his nose is rather small,
  Without a notion of a hook.

I wish he was a barrister,
Then he could talk and cause a stir,
And wear a lovely curly wig,
To make his face look brown and big;
A captain in a uniform
Might take a woman's heart by storm;
And sailors are the best of all,
Such charming partners at a ball:
But just a banker—don't you see,
  It is so very tame and flat—
Why *did* he want to marry me?
  How *could* Papa consent to that?

John Jerningham's a horrid name!
Alas! my cards must bear the same!

I do not think that it is wise
  Young men should be so spick and span;

John is so dreadfully precise,
He ought to be a clergyman!
He says I am untidy—he
Dislikes to see a hair astray,
And everything I use, you see,
He thinks I ought to put away.
He will not let me walk alone,
Studies he likes me still to con—
O, how I wish I was my own,
And never had belonged to John!

At breakfast it is rather nice—
Making the tea is like a play;
Only he gives me good advice,
And tells me how to spend the day.
At ten he goes—always at ten,
The most precise of business men:
At six I know he will return,
But rather stiff and taciturn,

Till dinner makes him kind and good—
  I think men look a little small,
They *do* depend so much on food,
  While we need hardly dine at all!

The dinner over, as I rise,
  He, leaning in his easy chair,
Regards me with approving eyes,
  Saying my muslin dress is fair.
But if he wants to kiss me, then
(Another tiresome way with men)
I pout—because it is no joke
Saluting lips perfumed with smoke.

To-night we're going to a ball;
  John says I must not dance too much—
John says I must not waltz at all—
  He thinks men murder with their touch!

At least I have a lovely dress,
  And when my hair is frizzled dry,
Done in a fashionable mess,
  It's quite the thing—and so am I!
I've got a charming little waist,
  And I can make it smaller yet;
John hates to see me tightly laced,
  But now and then I must forget!

My skirt is gored delightfully,
    With train so skilfully design'd,
It floats away three yards from me,
    While I sail on nor look behind.

. . . . . .

Well—it is over—let it go—
    When I was ready for the ball,
John said my dress was cut too low,
    And talked about a horrid shawl.
I felt that I should like to cry,
    So down I sat and tried to pout;
John fixed me with his steady eye,
    And said I should not go without.
Most kindly he remarked, 'You know
There's no occasion you *should* go!'
And then he gave a little laugh,
And fetched me my Chantilly scarf.

My robe was of another lace,
    And as he wrapped my shoulders round,

I thought if he but turned his face,
  I'd dash the thing upon the ground.

The room was splendid—hung with flags,
  And flow'rs as bright as they were sweet,
And all the ladies dressed in bags
  Straight from their waists down to their feet.
Fixed on John's arm, I moved about,
  And thought he might be more alert,
And wished some man would take me out,
  That I once more might dance and flirt.

The moonlight through the window came
  (I wonder if it likes a ball),
And laid itself in silver flame
  Across the floor and up the wall:
The dancers did not pause or start,
  Affrighted at its beauty sweet;
I think the girl can have no heart
  Who treads the moonlight 'neath her feet!

Invited by my host Sir James,
  I helped to form a prim quadrille.
He gaily told the people's names,
  And why some danced and some sat still.
To Lady Græme John took me then,
  And said, 'I'll leave you safely here:
I'm wanted by some other men
  To play a little rubber, dear!'
I did not tell him I was glad
  (I wonder if I was or no!)
Would he have minded if I had?
  I thought it cool of him to go,
So talked and laughed with Lady Græme—
  A pretty woman, kind and gay;
And she politely did the same,
  And so the moments slid away.

Up came a man I liked to see
Extremely—for he look'd at me.
Just six feet two (delightful height),
  With lazy eyes and classic nose,

And teeth that flashed, they were so white,
    And air of indolent repose,
And trailing whiskers, rather red,
But quite brown hair upon his head.
He sauntered up with languid air,
    To Lady Græme he murmured low,
'Aw—real-ly—aw—I don't much care—
    Aw—introduce me—don't you know?'
And with a glance politely free,
Just with his eyebrows signed at me.

The waltz is forming—off we go—
    How could I think of John's desire?
He danced divinely—to and fro,
    We whirl away and never tire.
The stately frizzle of my hair
    Just hung about a little bit.
My scarf? I'd left it on a chair,
    I'm sure I had no need of it—

Reflected from the shining glass,
I saw our charming figures pass,
And must confess I thought we were
A most *distingué*-looking pair.

Enraptured at the rapid flight,
My heart leapt up with new delight,
And sparkled in my lips and eyes,
And flushed my cheek with rosy dyes.
Gay words and gayer laughter sprang,
As round and round we lightly swang.
When in came John! appalling sight!
   Ah, John, you should have stayed away:
Is it the moonlight makes you white?
   Or is it passion kept at bay?

The naughty spirit seized me then,
Which makes us women tease the men.
As John stood scowling in the door,
I danced more wildly than before.

The music ceased, so cease we must,
  My partner bent and whispered praise,
John saw how he admir'd, I trust--
  He ne'er look'd so in all his days.

The roses on the window lay,
  And almost touch'd me as I stood.
They were as good as they were gay,
  Alas! I felt more gay than good!
Roses are very beautiful,
  And innocent, and sure to please:
But even roses would be dull
  Without their butterflies and bees!

Quite cool and pleasant, John came up,
  Offered his arm, and said 'twas late.
'I will not go before I sup.'
  'You must,' he cried, 'the horses wait.'

He held himself extremely high:
  I did not like his looks by half,
I think I'd have begun to cry,
  Only I felt inclin'd to laugh!
He wrapp'd me in the cloaking room,
With air of most portentous gloom;
No carriage waiting in the street,
  He called a cab, and off we went;
I kept on dancing with my feet,
  And felt too lively to repent.

Arrived at home, he paid the fare,
  In silence led me to my room,
In silence placed me in a chair,
  Then stood erect to speak my doom—
Saying in voice with anger fraught,
'I told you not to waltz, I thought.'

My spirit rose at being chid—
  And leaning languid in my chair

I answered, 'Did you?—so you did—
    It's late, I think—I'll brush my hair.'

O John! you frowned with such a frown,
I almost thought you'd knock me down,
And felt excited, pleased, and vext,
Wondering what was coming next.

Silent he stood—in silence looked—
And tho' my wrath I nursed and cooked,
It gave my heart a little turn,
That silence was so strangely stern.

Then with reproachful solemn face
He sat him in my writing place,
And took my paper, pen and ink—
Well, John, that's rather cool, I think!
And so he wrote and wrote and wrote—
    And I my ringlets brush and plait,
As he does up each tiny note,
    I wonder what he means by that!

He rings the bell, and Fanny knocks—
'Three letters for the letter-box!'
Then turns to me with tranquil air—
  'The summer-night has met the day,
You *must* have finish'd with your hair:
  But I have something still to say:
I shall not take you out at all
This spring to any other ball.
I've written notes to Mrs. Payne,
To Lady Vaux and Colonel Vane,
Explaining that we cannot go.'
'Oh John! you never have done so!'
'Of course I have!' his eyes flash light;
  'My wife to waltz I do not choose:
I've learned the task she taught to-night,
  Another lesson I refuse.'

'Oh John! you know—I never meant'—
'It is too late,' he said, and went.
And I, undrest, began to weep,
And fairly cried myself to sleep.

We met at breakfast—hard and cold
  Was John—and I was dignified—
I thought it was not right to scold
  And then shut up a six weeks' bride!
I read my letters, he the news,
  Calmly I handed him his tea,
And his politeness can't refuse
  To cut a slice of ham for me.
And now and then a look I slid
  Out of the corner of my eyes;
But glance at me, not once I did
  From this philosopher surprise,
And then I sighed—a little loud,
  And then I rattled with my cup,
But John read on serene and proud,
  And never once—not once—looked up!

He does not love me!—whence the thought,
Or why it came—or how it fell—
Or if I cared—or what I sought—
Or false or true I cannot tell.

He rose at ten to say good-bye,
I said it too—I think he sigh'd;
There *was* a trouble in his eye,
And I again felt dignified!

O dreary, dreary drawing-room,
Where never merry sound is heard—
O little chamber full of gloom,
The cage of a reluctant bird!

There is a shadow in the street:
There is a shadow on my heart.
O sky and grass you are so sweet:
O London house how sad thou art!

I feel the outer shadow creep
  To meet the shadow in my breast,
And shut my eyes or I should weep
  With such a weary sense of rest.

O could I stand beneath the sky,
  With shining grass about my feet,
And catch one bright blue butterfly:
  I think that life would be too sweet!

The shadows darken as I sit
  Around this home that is my own:
I feel a sudden fear of it,
  I am so lonely and alone.

How wearily the hours pass by,
  And yet the day is beautiful.
O *was* he sorry? *did* he sigh?
  O I am young, and life is dull!

It is no use that John should talk,
  How can I stay at home all day?
My head aches—I *must* take a walk,
  What harm can happen on the way?
Through half a dozen streets I run;
  All nicely dressed: free as the air:
Free as the wind: gay as the sun:
  If John is cross I will not care!

I enter on a lovely lawn,
  Where trees a happy shadow made;
I ask the name—almost in scorn,
  ''Tis Kensington,' the woman said.

O lovely lawn of Kensington,
  How very good and kind thou art,
To put such radiant colors on,
  To please one little longing heart!

Fair is the life by any led,
  That holds no brighter joy than this,
The pleasant sky above the head,
  And daisy buds the feet to kiss.

Who do I see beneath the trees?—
  Unless my vision plays me false,
That charming fellow sure to please—
  My partner in that wicked valse!

O garden full of new delight!—
  He says gay words; I make replies;
I know he is enchanted quite,
  And he admires me with his eyes:
We walk, we sit, we sit, we walk—
  O happy chance that brought us there!
How I enjoy his sprightly talk
  And knowledge that he thinks me fair!
He slyly hints with half a smile
  At how I vanished from the ball,

And lets me understand the while
 That when *I* went, joy went from all!
He's not a thing to do, I see,
 But talk to me 'neath summer sky;
The hours pass on, and so do we,—
 If he is happy, so am I.
I'm flirting just a little bit—
 But flirting keeps a girl alive:
I turn my watch and look at it—
 I almost scream—'tis half-past five!

I go in haste—he sees me home;
 I beg him not—he says he will:
I'm so afraid lest John should come;
 The terror almost makes me ill.
When Westbourne Terrace is in sight
 I stop him firmly, once for all,
To persevere he's too polite,
 But begs to be allowed to call:

I faintly murmur, 'Number eight';
    He shakes my hand with tender touch,
And laughing cries, 'I see you're late—
    I fear the husband scolds too much!'

O grand escape! I'm barely in
    When John comes knocking to the door;
I feel as if I'd sinned a sin,
    I never felt so strange before.

At dinner John is solemn still;
    I'm too excited far to eat,
But John would eat or well or ill
    (Men never seem to turn from meat,
Their dinner never comes amiss).
    When to the drawing-room I go
He does not ask me for a kiss—
    He does not care for me, I know!
How can I tell him that I did
The very thing he most forbid?—

I think he'll kill me; but I'll try,
I hope I could not act a lie.

In stately pride our tea we drink,
Now is the time to speak, I think;
But John speaks first, 'Pray, have you read
The book I marked for you?' he said.
'I? no; I never opened it;
You spend your time as you think fit.'
Grimly he answered, 'Will you play
The symphony you learned to-day?'
'I did not learn one.' 'Ah, indeed,
You did not care to play or read;
What *did* you do?' What *could* I say?
  Tell him the truth I never can,
Which is—I walked about all day
  With an extremely pleasant man!
And so I murmur, 'Many things,'
And from my fingers pull the rings.

John looks at me, I look at him—
His eye is stern, and mine is dim:
He takes a book—some pamphlet light,
Nor says another word that night.

3

He called to-day—sent up two cards;
  For the first time I learned his name—
Arthur Fitzmaurice, of the Guards:
  O how I wish John's was the same!
I thought I must not let him in—
Visits from men John holds a sin,
Unless he's present when they call,
To make the talk political:
But just as 'Not at home,' I cry,
His entrance is his sole reply—
So easy, smiling, tall, and gay,
I'm charmed he did not go away.

I chatter like a merry girl;
  He talks of half a hundred things—

Of how to wear the latest curl,
  Of how divinely Nilsson sings,
Of how the Prince upon the Nile
Has bravely bagged his crocodile,
While Ministers will hardly dare
To bag a paltry Irish *mare;*
Of how no fellow in the land
Would undertake to understand
Or for the hidden meanings look
That give its *weight* to Browning's 'Book,'
While beauties stare him in the face
In every line of 'Lady Grace,'
And 'tis a work of love alone
To make those beauties all his own.

Each little word is slyly meant
To introduce a compliment,
And show (although he does not stare)
He thinks me pretty, nice, and fair,—

Just in the way some people can—
The way that makes a pleasant man!

Ah, as we speak the present flies,
And forms the past before our eyes!
With half a smile and half a sigh,
So earnest is his last good-bye,
That Juliet's words I could repeat,
And own the pain of parting sweet.

A fortnight since a word I writ!
　Each day was beautiful and kind,
But, somehow, when I'd done with it
　It left a little sting behind.

I can't believe that they are wrong—
　The converse sweet and merry walk:
Why should I have my legs and tongue
　If 'tis a sin to run and talk?

I wish I'd let John truly know,
　But then the meetings he'd forbid,
And shut me up and scold me so,
　And be annoyed at all I did.

If Arthur was my husband, then
I'd never talk with other men,
A *tête-à-tête* with him would be
The most enchanting chat for me—
He is so charming and refined,
And all I say he seems to mind;
So 'tis not that I could not prove
Good wife to husband that I love;
But that *my* husband's not the one
I can like best beneath the sun.
Why, since the evening of the ball
He hardly spoke to me at all
Until last night, all suddenly,
He sat him down and lectured me:
He call'd me headstrong, giddy, wild,
And chid me like a naughty child,
Then spoke of meekness, patience, faith,
The woman he could love till death,
'The perfect woman, nobly planned,
To warn, to comfort, and command.'

'*I'm* ready to command,' I said;
And then I cried and hung my head:
He asked me did I love him? what
Could I reply?—I answered not!
And then he stared in sudden gloom,
And stalked about and left the room.

Why did he marry me? I see
He does not care a bit for me!
Ah, if he did, he would not scold,
Nor wish me to be dull and old;
His happy love would gild my days
With glances fond and tender praise;—
A petted Queen, I'd shine on all,
And then—ah, me!—I'd give a ball:
I softly ask'd him if I might
  (By Arthur's generous advice);
His answer was uncivil quite—
  O John, your manners are not nice!

And Arthur says men should not reign,
That is the woman's place, 'tis plain;
And Arthur says such eyes as mine
  Would change to day the darkest night,
And those who think such eyes divine
  Are those for whom they wear their light.

To lock the sunlight in a room,
  Trying to make it shine by rule,
And keep the outer world in gloom,
  Would be the action of a fool;
And he who'd shut *me* up alone,
  Nor let me fling about my rays,
But keep me only for his own
  Is just as silly, Arthur says.

You plant a lily in a cave—
  Poor, pretty thing, it can but die;
You would enchain the ocean wave—
  It dares you as it dances by!

It mocks you with its ceaseless foam,
  Your dripping heads you fain would free,
And little laughters slyly come
  For him who would enchain the sea.

And I must gently fade away,
  And like the lily end my days,
Or like the waves be brave and gay,
  And spurn my fetters, Arthur says.

And day by day the days glide on,
  And I glide on and cannot stay;
I wonder if the busy sun
  Is tired of always making day!

Weary with an excess of light,
  I think he holds the dark a boon;
I think he'd like to see the night,
  And would enjoy to be the moon!

O change, I hold you best of all;
  Nothing is good that must remain;
Vanish my street—my houses fall,
  And let me be a girl again!

To-night we dined with Lady Græme;
I wore my skyblue silk—the same
At Mrs. Payne's I'd meant to wear,
Had John allowed me to be there.
Fanny my hair did well enough,
Over a most triumphant puff.
It rose a yard above my head,
Crowned by a wreath of roses red.

Sir James, goodhumored, frank, and gay,
Received us in his pleasant way,
And cried 'At half a dozen balls,
  And all in vain, I've sought your face:
Believe me, in those garnished halls
  None shone with such a saucy grace—
Alas, why do you stay away?
Youth is the time to make your play.'

I answer'd coolly, 'Yes—'tis so—
My husband will not let me go,
All invitations he's refused.'
John blushed at that, and looked confused,
But I was glad that he should see
His dear Sir James thought much of me.
'Twas a large party—we were late!
  Sir James said, 'Ring the dinner bell
For one young man we will not wait.
  Arthur's a most uncertain swell.'
The door flew open as he spoke—
  'Captain Fitzmaurice' said the man,
I almost thought it was a joke,
  And little shivers through me ran.

I bit my lips and sat upright;
  I blushed and felt extremely hot;
He bowed to me with air polite,
  Looking as if he saw me not—
Nodded at others, smiled to some,
And said, 'Aw—aw—I'm glad I've come!'

When good Sir James, as bridal guest,
  Politely gave his arm to me,
I thought that he must be in jest;
  For I forgot my dignity.
It seemed so strange that I should go
Heading the grand procession so.

The table was extremely gay
  With little heaps of fruit and flow'rs,
And all the dinner hid away,
  And eating it took two good hours.
Arthur sat opposite to me,
And never seemed my face to see;
Asking the lady at his side,
'Aw—really—is that girl a bride?'

I thought it wrong to make pretence
With such a show of innocence,
And something whispered very low.
John never would have acted so!

The ladies to the drawing-room go,
  'Tis deadly lively there, I own;
Why is it so extremely slow,
  When women find themselves alone?
We sit about and mildly chat,
  Each sips and stirs her coffee cup;
But conversation's rather flat,
  We want the men to brisk us up.

They come, and round my chair they crowd,
  My spirits rise, my heart is free;
Some murmur low, some chatter loud;
  And all that's said is said to me.
I bandy repartee and wit,
  With smiles their nonsense I reward,
Whatever's said I answer it,
  And all I say the men applaud!

John stands and talks to Lady Græme,
  Unsympathetic, calm, and cool;

But then John always is the same,
  To care for *that* I'd be a fool.

But Arthur gnaws his handsome lip,
  And looks with thunder in his eyes;
While careless I my coffee sip,
  Smiling in innocent surprise!

'Tis charming to attract and please,
But still more sweet it is to tease.

Ah! he approaches—listlessly—
  Dropping a sentence here and there—
Looking at prints he does not see—
  Pretending not to see my chair—
Stopping a moment to address
  Some one he hardly saw or knew.
—I know that manner purposeless,
  That always has an end in view!

He leaned upon my chair and said,
  'When shall we have another valse?'
His whiskers almost touch my head—
  I'm glad my chignon was not false!

I try to speak, but I am dumb!
  'Tis this concealment makes me shy—
Instead of words, hot blushes come;
  Arthur may triumph now—not I!

Softly my drooping glance I raise,
To meet Sir James's wond'ring gaze!
All out of countenance I rise;
  I know not what I say or do—
There's such amazement in his eyes,
  And something like reproval too!

Where is my self-possession? O!
  I should not have jumped up like this!
(I wish I was unmarried tho';
  Then flirting never came amiss)!

'Sit down,' said Arthur in my ear,
And down I sat abashed and weak;
I wish I had not felt that fear—
I wish I'd had the wit to speak!

Uncounted thoughts come rushing in,
My self-approval to destroy;
And every thought is like a sin,
And every sin is like a joy.
Deceit is such an ugly word—
I did not utter the untrue—
John's strictness really is absurd;
O John, the fault is all with you!
Life is so innocent and sweet,
I must be happy, and I will!
My youth is lying at my feet;
Can I the radiant creature kill?
Must I blot out the perfect sun?
Fling the unopen'd buds away?
Nor let the silver river run?
My heart leaps up and *will* be gay.

My life is such a lovely game,
　It charms me ere I understand,
With little joys, like birds, so tame,
　They come a-flying to my hand.
Why am I shamefaced and perplexed?
　And why is John so cross and grave?
And why with Arthur am I vexed?
　Why am I not serenely brave?

Then Arthur whispered, 'How you blush!'
　I answered angrily, 'Don't talk—
You must not call again—and—hush—
　I'll never meet you when I walk.'
'Alas!' he cried, 'but then—'tis true—
You can't prevent *my* meeting *you!*'

I tried to look a little grim,
　But down he sat and rattled on;
My ready laughter answered him;
　My fears are fled—my grief is gone.

He talked in such a pleasant strain,
With tones so soft and wit so bright,
I was my merry self again,
And quite forgot my foolish fright.

I wore a rosebud in my dress,
He vowed for him that bud should shine,
(Just fancy John in such distress
For anything because 'tis mine!)
I held the rosebud in the air,
And uttered half a dozen noes.
He said than me it was less fair;
I told him that MY name was Rose.
He caught my hand—he snatched the flower,
Kissed it, and laid it 'neath his vest,
Saying that from that happy hour
He'd always love the roses best.
The million stars that deck the skies
Have no such meaning for his eyes,

Nor priceless gems such joy impart
As one small rosebud on his heart.

Sir James approached me very grave,
Enquired coldly, would I sing?
His altered looks I laughing brave,
And could not think of such a thing!
Like sentry at my side he stood,
And all the pleasant chat is o'er.
I think Sir James is very good,
But just a little of a bore.
John took me home grave as a judge;
No word was spoken on the way;
He seems to owe me quite a grudge;
He's always sulky when I'm gay.

. . . . .

. . . . .

Wrapped in a peignoir fresh and clear,
I view my face and find it fair.
John enters then, and standing near
Watches me while I brush my hair.

'Rose, do you ever think at all?'
'Oh yes,' I said, 'I often do;
I think I'd like to give a ball,
And not to be reproved by you.'
'But do you ever think of life,
How great it is—how fair might be;
And of the duties of a wife,
And kind submission due to me?'

A troop of little thoughts like sighs,
All uninvited fill my breast;
Sweet little thoughts of woods and skies,
And moments fetterless and blest.;

'And do *you* ever think,' I cry,
'That duties also fall to you,
And since you chose to wed me—why
You ought to make me happy too?'

He viewed me sternly where he stood—
'Ah, Rose! your life might joy impart,

If you were gentle, kind, and good,
With woman's wisdom in your heart.'

I twisted round each glossy curl,
I mocked him with my saucy eyes:
'I'm not a woman, but a girl—
I'd rather far be fair than wise!'

'Time is so pitiless,' he said;
'Shall time be pitiless in vain?
When youth is fled and beauty dead,
What will remain?—what will remain?'

Laughing, I cried, 'Ah! see the foal,
It scours the field, it can't keep still,
The kitten—little merry soul—
For ever plays, for ever will;
The horse is steady, and the cat
Is dull as you can wish, I'm sure;
She sits all day upon the mat,
And licks her paws and looks demure.

'Oh, let me while I'm young be gay,
  Just to be happy never hurts;
When I am old I'll sit all day,
  And read your books and mend your shirts!'

I let my golden hair run down,
  And on the ground its beauty trail;
And, as an answer to his frown,
  Laughed at him through the shining veil.

With angry grasp my arm he took—
  His temper from its bondage broke.
'I *will not* let you speak and look
  As but to-night you looked and spoke.'

Strange shadow flits athwart his brow,
  Strange light makes glitter in his eyes,
A moody passion shakes him now,
  The shadow's gone—the glitter dies.

His face my spirit *shall* not daunt,
I *will* not let him win the day,
So give my voice a little taunt,
And smiling up at him, I say,
'You'd like to beat me.' 'Yes, I would,'
He cried, 'my anger I'd restrain,
But if I thought 'twould do you good
I'd beat you now and yet again!
In marriage there are double lives,
Where each to each must law allow;
Men have a right to beat their wives
When women break their marriage vow.'
'*I* break my vow?' 'Yes, every day.'
He turned to where I breathless sat,
'You swore to honor and obey.'
'O dear!' I cried, 'who thinks of *that?*'

'Think of it now you must and can,'
And answer ere you leave this place—
Why did you blush to meet that man!
How dared you flirt before my face?'

'What man?' asked I. He did not stir;
  And so I softly cried—'Alack!
And would you really, John, prefer
  That I should flirt behind your back?'

He grasped my arm—my arm is small—
  He left a mark—(I see it now)
And cried, 'You shall not flirt at all,
  A glance may break a marriage vow!
I ask you where you met that man?'
  How hard I strove to get away!
Tell him the truth I never can:
  Ah, foolish girl! what can I say?

'I will not speak—ah, John, you hurt—
  Ah, let me go.' 'Then answer quick.'
My heart beat fast—no longer pert,
  I trembled, wept, felt faint and sick.

'Where did you meet that man before?'
  'Ah, John, 'tis hard.' 'I do not care,

I will not let you pass that door
  Till you have answered me, I swear.'

'I met him at Sir James's ball.'
  'Where else?' 'I don't remember—I—'
'Where else?' 'Ah, nowhere else at all.'
  'I fear' quoth he, 'you've told a lie.'

And so he went!—I cried all night,
  Sitting defenceless in the cold,
Crying with sorrow and affright,
  And horror at the lie I'd told.

I meant no harm those pleasant days,
  'Twas the excitement led me on;
I liked the flattery and praise,
  Things that I never get from John.

It was so sweet to wander out,
  And then I was afraid to tell;

If John had let me run about
   And chatter it had all been well!

I sought my bed with weeping eyes,
   When morning broke and housemaids stirred.
At breakfast time I could not rise—
   John left the house without a word.

And all that day I stayed within,
And mused with horror on my sin;
And little did I do but cry—
I never thought I'd tell a lie!
I felt relief in my distress,
When I determined to confess;
To speak the truth to John once more
Would bring a calm unknown before.

But then my aching eyes I hid,
  Thinking how great his wrath would be;
I'd done all things that he forbid,
  And let a man make love to me!

Perhaps he'd beat me! once again
  I was a child in shame and fear,

I knew the terror and the pain,
    And thought John's hand would be severe.
I pushed my sleeve, made bare the mark
    That dumbly threatened future harm:
Four little shadows—lightly dark—
    Laid on the whiteness of my arm.

As on my boudoir couch I lay
My thoughts seemed melting quite away;
Slow and more slow the fancies crept,
I shut my eyes—I think I slept.

I dream that I am in a wood;
    There is a rustling 'mid the leaves:
A robin comes to seek his food,
    A happy thing that never grieves.
Is it the color on his breast
    That makes a robin's heart so light?
Or is it that we love him best
    And praise him when he's out of sight?

The rustling wakes me—some one's near,
Whose eye my sleeping face regards;
I see with quite a pang of fear
Captain Fitzmaurice of the Guards!

My hair is hanging all astray
(If John had seen it, he'd complain),
I had been crying half the day,
I felt I *must* be looking plain!
That's my first thought—my second is
I'm wishing to be good and true:
John would be quite enraged at this,
Why *did* he come?—what *shall* I do?

He shakes my hand—my arm is bare,
The open sleeve the mark displays,
He cries, 'The villain! did he dare?'
His lazy eyes are in a blaze,
A little kiss is on my hand,
I hang my head and blush with shame,

Wishing to make him understand
  That John is not so much to blame.

While thus we stand the door's flung wide,
John enters with a haughty stride,
The rightful master of the place,
With dreadful anger in his face.

I snatched my hand from Arthur—ran
  To John; 'I was asleep,' I cried,
And he looked at me as *he* can
  And as no other can beside!

Coolly he turned to Arthur (then
  I quite admired him), calm his tone:
'There's some mistake, sir—gentlemen
  Don't call here when my wife's alone.'

On Arthur's face there broods a frown;
  'A gentleman I think I'm styled—

Your wife's the prettiest girl in town—
 Are you a man to beat this child?'

'*I* beat her?' John with scorn replied—
 (I wonder did he recollect
His little lecture when he cried
 Men should chastise and wives respect?)
With lordly air he paced the floor
 And said, 'I'll have no words of strife,
Captain Fitzmaurice—there's the door—
 No man shall meddle with my wife.'

Captain Fitzmaurice blushed at this,
 And cried, 'No child's more innocent,
And guileless as a child she is,'
 And then he bowed to me and went.

I somehow felt quite proud of John,
 I liked his cool, determined ways;
We were alone—Fitzmaurice gone;
 John looked at me—I hid my face.

Now I must speak, or not at all,
  I need not wait for strength to come,
So spoke, beginning at the ball
  And ending with this day at home:
I told him how I broke his laws,
  And let each day its pleasure bring,
And how I liked to flirt, because
  I found it such a pleasant thing;
How we had met outside the door,
  And how he called upon me here,
And how I tried to speak before,
  And how I lied to him from fear.

And when I had confessed my sin,
  I felt so desolate and poor,
And drew my little shoulders in,
  Thinking, 'He'll beat me now, I'm sure.'

He spoke no word, he made no sign,
  My breath came fast, my heart beat thick;

I thought, if this were wife of mine
  I'd beat her and forgive her quick.
Slow speech at last—'You told a lie,
  I doubt whate'er your tongue asserts,
I have no faith in falsehood, I,
  Nor yet in faithless, fickle flirts!'
Out burst his wrath: 'I gave you trust;
  I loved—O God, I was deceived!
My love is shattered in the dust:
  Can I believe as I believed?'

Half fainting on the wall I lean,
  I never knew my heart so stirred;
Oh, if each stroke had only been
  A blow, and not a cruel word!
I cannot speak, I cannot cry,
  I am so dull and turned to stone;
I hear a sound, a step, and I
  Am in the chamber all alone.

He came not near me all the day,
He came not near me all the night;
I almost wept my life away
In sorrow, penitence, and fright.
A letter's brought—what can it be?
A manly hand—I know it well,
He wrote two little notes to me
When I was only Rosa Bell.

Ah, were I Rosa Bell again,
And once again he made me wife,
He'd have no reason to complain,
I'd lead so excellent a life!
Why is it ever just too late,
When what was living is a ghost
We cease to quarrel with our fate,
And what is lost could prize the most?

THE LETTER.

'I LEAVE my home this night for Spain,
And though for ever must remain
The sin, the sorrow, and the stain,
If time my feelings should constrain,
And take the anger from the pain,
In time I may return again.'

The letter fluttered from my hand,
I hardly seemed to understand;
Startled, bewildered, and confused,
My eyes to teach my brain refused.

For Spain?—I knew that sunny clime
  Some claim upon his house could lay—
A trouble of the troubled time,
  To vanish with a brighter day;

And he had meant to seek her skies,
  And for a little while remain,
Just when he first beheld my eyes,
  And bade a blithe good-bye to Spain.
An apt pretence the mission made
  To leave the love his lips disown;
And I, repentant and afraid,
  Weep o'er that ruined love alone.

That night Sir James sent in his card,
Saying it was a business call;
He bowed with such a stiff regard,
I trembling felt he knew of all:
He told me Mr. Jerningham
Had asked him to arrange affairs,
'And so,' he mutter'd, 'here I am,'
And ran his fingers through his hairs.

Bending my head I could not speak,
Trying to swallow down my tears,
Wondering how I'd grown so weak—
A day had done the work of years!

'While he's abroad, he settles it
That you should sojourn by the sea,

With some companion, as is fit—
  But where and who ?—How shall it be ?'

'Whate'er you please,' I faintly said,
  Viewing my life with vacant stare;
My life !—I was already dead,
  And might be buried anywhere?

'So be it; I'll arrange it all,
  And choose a place that's free from crowd;
To-morrow, if I may, I'll call
  At half-past two;' he stiffly bowed.

My heart was ice, my face was flames—
  I said, 'Oh won't you say "good-bye"?
Won't you shake hands with me, Sir James?'
  And bitterly began to cry.

The kind, good creature seized my hand—
  'Crying,' he said, 'does good to none;

I'd really like to understand,
  Poor little thing, what *have* you done?'

I told him all, from first to last—
So grave his looks my tears fell fast,
And I accepted my disgrace,
Reading my sentence in his face.

He whistled very soft and low,
  And cried, 'It *is* a precious mess;
How could you treat your husband so?
  He'll not forgive you soon, I guess!
Youth, beauty, health, friends not a few,
  An easy income, pleasant lot,
A noble fellow fond of you—
  What *could* you want you had not got?
To shatter such a life to bits!
  And all for what?—for nothing! or
To let that foolish fellow, Fitz,
  Say things he should be horsewhipped for!

'Pray, do you know the use of life?
That no one's life is his alone?
Or what it is to be a wife
And call a good man's love your own?
And to be trusted with a trust—
Trusted and yet to be untrue;
To lay his honor in the dust
And break a heart that beats for you?"

Each word he said appeared a law
That if accepted might restore,
And each a picture seemed to draw
Of beauty never known before.
I caught a glimpse of Paradise—
Of lovely order, pleasure fit!
And then I hid my weeping eyes
Because I was shut out of it!

'And such a man as John—by Jove,
A woman might adore that man!

He loved you with a real love,
As only real fellows can!
How dared you play with life like that,
Making a trifle of a sin?—
Child! did you know what you were at,
Or half the danger you were in?'

'Danger? Ah yes!' I sadly cry—
'I've lost my husband's love, 'tis plain,
And told him such a wicked lie
We never can be friends again.'

He stared at me. 'Is that the whole?'—
While yet he frowned he almost smiled,
And softly said, 'God bless my soul!
How could John marry such a child?'
And then, with quite a tender look
(Cause for the change I could not find),
He talked like fathers in a book—
Papa was never half so kind.

'You have been frivolous and vain,
 But yet I think your heart is good;
I think you will not err again,
 I think you'll learn what women should:
And so, for fear the world should blame,
 And mingle falsehood with the truth,
I'll take you home to Lady Græme,
 And we'll protect your foolish youth!'

PART II.

THREE bitter months have passed away.
  I could not—could not write a line:
But in the welkin dim and gray
  A little star begins to shine.

A little star—though not for me,
  Still by its light I wander on;
It *was* a sort of joy to see
  A letter to Sir James from John!

Oh, sort of joy, how sad I am!—
  He says he comes to-night, tho' late.
And 'hopes that Mrs. Jerningham
  Will be at home at Number eight.'

So I'm to live with him again!—
  It is his will to have it so;
Oh dreadful pleasure!—happy pain!
  Oh senseless joy!—too real woe!

I cross the threshold of the door,
  How sad I am—how changed is all!—
Am I the girl who oft before
  Ran up the steps and through the hall?

If I am not that creature gay,
  I hope I'm something better far;—
Shine in the welkin dim and gray,
  Though not for me, my little star!

I sit beside the silent fire,
  The passing minutes work their will,
I have no wishes or desire,
  I never felt so very still.

I think I have wept out my tears,
For future grief can none allow;
I've lost the knack of hopes and fears,
And am a quiet woman now.

He likes a woman full of grace,
By reason's law her heart to quell—
(Why did he like my happy face
When I was only Rosa Bell?)

I see a girl's face in the glass,
All light and shadow, smiles and tears;
Alas, it is my own! alas!
And am I still what *that* appears?

He will not like me! Ah, I thought
My heart had learned in sorrow's school,
And, once the teacher, now the taught,
Had ruled my face with iron rule!

He will not like me! Oh despair!
　　To meet him with such changeful eyes?
Ah! face that I believed so fair,
　　Can you not look a *little* wise?

Alas! a distant sound I hear;
　　The cruel moments reel and fly;
It is his step, and he is here—
　　If I could hide away and die!

. . . . . .

I stood so friendless in the room,
　　I felt so lonely and afar;
The house was filled so full of gloom,
　　I could not see my little star!

John entered—shook me by the hand,
　　And said, 'How cold the weather is!
The train was late, I understand.'
　　This was our meeting—only this!

I said 'the train is always slow;'
   And then I laughed—indeed I did—
Tho' what I meant I do not know;
   Nor how the laughter from me slid.

He called it cold, and I was hot;
   I longed to look at him, but feared—
One glance I gave, and saw he'd got
   Upon his chin a great black beard.

I saw no higher—I was dumb—
   I vaguely wondered, *was* it he?
Or had some bearded Spaniard come
   To pass himself as John on me?
I did not dare to look again—
   How could I tell if it was John?
Never, unless I looked, 'tis plain—
   And so my foolish thought ran on!
I wondered did he glance at me?
   And did he find me beautiful?

And then I poured him out his tea;
  And there we sat so cold and dull.

'How is Sir James?' 'He's very well.'
  'And Lady Græme?' 'She's better too.'
'Has she been ill?' 'I cannot tell—
  O yes—I mean—she did—you knew.'

And then I stopped and turned from John—
  And colored up and bit my lips,
And played a little tune upon
  The table with my finger tips.
John gazed intently in his cup,
  And spoke with kindness in his tone:
(Why did my heart at once freeze up,
  And wish he'd left me quite alone?)
'They have been good to you?' 'Oh yes,
  Sir James is all that's good and kind,
And Lady Græme—I like her less;
  But she is pleasant and refined.'

I spoke with fluency and ease,
   I felt provoked—I know not why;
John stirred his tea and crossed his knees,
   And did not make the least reply.
And then I wished I had not spoke,
   And wondered what would happen next.
And then the clock gave forth its stroke.
   'Twas twelve—he rose—and I was vexed.
'Good night,' he said. 'Good night,' said I—
   (How could we hope for a good night ?)
He left me—I sat down to cry,
   And of his face I'd had no sight!

At breakfast it was just the same,
  But I looked at him, bolder grown—
One little look—when, full of shame,
  I met his eyes, and dropped my own:
His face was stern and resolute,
  His mouth was hard as cut in steel;
Cold were his eyes, yet from them shoot
  Looks that my very soul must feel.
He is my husband—once he loved;
  His heart *was* mine, and might be still:
It was my hand, his hand removed,
  That would have sheltered me from ill;
I asked my heart—could his be stirred,
  That love once slighted to restore?
And still my heart replied one word,
  And still that word was Nevermore!

And when the clock was striking ten,
  He rose—I felt a dreamlike fear;
O most precise of business men—
  He's gone—but was he ever here?
Is it a dream? am I alive?
  Has life begun again for us?
And *can* I live—howe'er I strive,
  In such a dreadful fashion thus?

Through all that night I had not slept:
    In cushion'd chair I languid lay,
Nor knew that slumber softly stepped,
    And drew the outer world away;
And when the twilight's tender gloom
    Gave shadows like primeval trees,
I felt the sounds within the room,
    And then I felt the sounds were these.

'She was a welcome guest, you know—'
    'Your kindness will be ne'er forgot—'
'And she's a charming creature, tho'
    She has her faults—and who has not?'

'Your pardon—tho' our friendly lives
    Have known each other long—what then?

Men do not talk about their wives,
And their wives' faults with other men.'

'Tut tut—your words I shall not heed;
My love of chat you will not balk:
John, I must speak—I must indeed;
Be a good fellow—let me talk:
I lectur'd her too—on my life,
She took it sweetly—ne'er forgot:
And John, altho' she *is* your wife,
I was her friend when you were not!'

'I acted for the best, Sir James,
And think I did extremely right—
Pray have you seen the members' names
Who voted for the Church last night?'

'Confound the Church!—you needn't frown;
I say you were too hard with *her;*
You should have let her see the town,
And shop, and dance, as girls prefer.

'Your wife's a beauty—others see,
  And tell her—and she knows 'tis true.
John, if you'll be advised by me,
  You'll let her hear the same from you.
With rosy cheeks and shining curls
  You fell in love—for all your nous:
Men should not marry little girls,
  Who want old women in the house!'

'Sir James, when I require advice,
  I'll ask for it, as custom is—
Pardon me, I may be too nice,
  But I'm a trifle tired of this.'
'I'll do my duty—say my say—
  We had her for three months with us.
She's young and skittish—fond of play—
  A little vain and frivolous—
Most women are—shall men condemn?
  Let us be wise and reason thus—
We'd better make the best of them,
  As—bless their hearts—they do of us!

'Don't leave your wife too much alone;
Just to amuse and please her try.
John, you've a temper of your own;
Don't frighten her, and make her cry!
She's a fine creature—good at heart,
Without a particle of vice;
And if she shies or tries to start,
Don't pull the curb—that's *my* advice!'

'Advice not asked for nor required;
Thank you—I'll manage as before;
I think I'm just a little tired;
Sir James, excuse me, there's the door!'

'With all my heart, and welcome too!
From no man's house I'm turned out twice;
You managed nicely—didn't you?
You stuck-up fellows scorn advice!'

The door was slammed, and all was still—
John stood erect—I feared him most;
But left my chair against my will,
And glided forward like a ghost.

John started—'*You?*' 'I was asleep;'
Ah, once before those words I said!
Strange memories through my bosom creep:
John feels them too—his cheek is red—

'I heard a little—he meant well—
I'm sorry you have quarrelled—he
Was kinder than my words can tell;
And all my faults he told to me.'

'You *did* not like to hear your faults,'
Said John, 'you thought the thing ill-bred.'
'I'm—altered—now,' with little halts,
The words came out—and they are said!

He looked at me with steady look,
　And then as steadily replied,
'I'm glad to hear it'—took a book—
　Lighted the lamp and read—I sighed.

A little week has crept away,
  We live together—John and I—
Just in the same too dreadful way—
  But I feel ill—I hope I'll die!

Would he be sorry if I died?
  Ah, yes—for once he loved me well;
Ah, yes—for once he did not chide,
  When I was only Rosa Bell!

Those happy days would come again,
  He would forget my foolish sin,
Forget the sorrow and the pain—
  The dead such sweet remembrance win.

Would he plant flowers on my grave?
His tears upon the blossoms fall?
And wear the golden ring he gave?
Alas! my finger is so small!

He'd say, 'She was so young and fair,
She was so gay and fond of life;'
And then he'd kiss the bit of hair
Cut from the head of his dead wife.

I think it would be sweet to die,
If held in memory so fair;
I'd like within my grave to lie,
'Neath little buds he planted there.

I'd like to live within his breast,
And feel, as years their softness shed,
That all his anger is at rest—
I know he'll love me when I'm dead!

Ah! shall I lie remember'd thus,
  If death's cold hand shall draw me hence:
Or—will he call me 'frivolous,'
  And wed a woman full of sense?

I hate that woman—well I know
  The sort of things she'll say and do;
I don't believe he'll like her, tho';
  Women like her are liked by few.

Ah! once he lov'd me—now forgot,
  The passion that his heart did move,
And when he lov'd—I lov'd him not—
  And now he loves me not—I love!

Last night I told him Mrs. Grey
   Invited me to drive with her,
And said she'd call on Saturday—
   'What should I do?' 'What you prefer.'
'I'd like to go with her.' 'Then go—
   My wish to interfere is gone,
Unless for something that I *know*
   'Tis better you should leave alone.'

I clasped my hands—I stood upright—
   Whence courage came I never knew—
'John, I am anxious to *do right*,
   And to obey your wishes too.'

The speech is made! what will he say?
   Will he my penitence disdain?

O how I longed to run away,
  Or be my naughty self again!

I thought his voice was grave and sad
  (Why should he *grieve* at such a plan?),
As he replied, 'I'm very glad,
  And I will help you if I can.'

Then it was over—there we sat
  Without a word to say at all!
I, working stitches on my mat,
  He, staring at the painted wall.
But mine is not a silent tongue,
  Its words are wing'd for sudden flight;
I often chatter when it's wrong,
  And can't keep silence when it's right.
And so I cried, 'O if you will
  I'll find it easy to be good:
There's such a charm in doing ill,
  It cannot always be withstood!'

'You think so?' I had meant no harm
And found his satire hard to bear—
'Such women somehow find a charm
In all that's excellent and fair.'

'Well—say I am not one of these,'
And from his tone my tone I took,
'Some women find it hard to please,
And some—give pleasure by a look!'

I looked at him—Ah foolish girl,
Whose vanity no slighting brooks,
'Before a swine don't cast your pearl:'
Said he, 'I do not care for looks!
You heard that foolish fellow Græme
Tell me to praise your air and grace;
But faith I won't! it is a shame
To praise a woman to her face!'

'I do not care for praise,' I cry,
  'I wonder if you're saying sooth?'
A quick repentance fires his eye;
  He had not meant to taunt my truth.
My ready blushes point the sting.
  I ply my needle very fast;
O when will memory cease to bring
  These bitter voices from the past?

He spoke—his tone was soft and low,
  His words I never can forget.
'You told me the whole truth, I know,
  That morning—when—when last we met.'
'I did,' I whispered, 'and I meant
  To tell it had you not come in,
For I was really penitent,
  Determined to confess my sin.
I did not only speak because—
  Because—' I stammered—thought of Fitz—

'Did you believe me then?'—a pause—
  'Well—no—or only little bits—
When I came home I was more wise,
  A moment did my soul convince,
For then—I looked into your eyes,
  And have believed you ever since!'

My heart is lighter in my breast,
  A little lighter—ah not much!
I think some pain has been carest,
  And laid asleep by tender touch.
I think a terror is forgot—
  A bitter voice has ceased to speak,
A tiny hope where hope was not
  Is shining like a glowworm meek.

Our hearts are drawn a little near,
  Our words come forth a little free,
I feel for him a shade less fear,
  And he a shade less wrath for me.

He knows I'm wishing for the light,
  He knows I know he knows I'm true,

He knows his hand can guide me right,
I know he knows I know it too!

And through it all one little gleam
Shines likes a dawn where suns might rise—
O did I hear it in a dream,
Or did he really praise my eyes?
I care not if 'tis good or wise,
But I my sweetest comfort take,
Because he looked into my eyes,
And has believed me for their sake.

And in my heart he fixed a sting,
That lurks in its remoter nooks,
Vexing me more than anything—
He said he did not care for looks!

Another ball! He took me there,
He knew I'd keep his waltzing laws;
I put some lilies in my hair,
And wore a dress of shining gauze.
I'm growing very old and wise,
My vanity is gone, I see—
I only care to please *his* eyes,
And that is not from vanity!

We enter—people turn to gaze,
And utter little sounds of praise:
Sweet sounds to please a lover's ear
(Alas, how sweet to be so dear!)
I feel the blushes on my cheek—
I glance at him' subdued and shy—
O silent face that will not speak,
Impenetrable lip and eye!

A dozen partners claim my hand,
I yield to each polite command;
I dance quadrilles, to waltz I long,
But pleasant things are always wrong!
That lovely whirling through the air,
    That tuneful racing with the feet,
I hold a thing divinely fair,
    What other exercise so sweet?
Three times I danced with Captain Groom,
    A pleasant partner, gay and nice,
He took me to the supper room,
    And brought me little cakes and ice.
A feathered fan I've left behind,
    He flies for it, my loss confest,
Myself quite by myself I find,
    The happy waltz detains the rest.

'Rose of the world!' a voice I hear—
    I turn—I start—I almost scream—

Fitzmaurice whispers in my ear,
 And takes my hand—is it a dream?
Too startled to be dignified,
 Or show a particle of sense,
I just looked at him and I cried,
 'O don't!' my folly was immense!

'O don't? O do—' he said and smiled,
 His lazy eyes are strangely bright,
'O Rose that hast my heart beguiled,
 Be just a little kind to-night.
He shall not hurt you—trust to me—
 I'll save you from that wicked John,
To-morrow may I hope to see
 A lovely Rose in Kensington?'

He smiled with that bewitching air,
 He murmured in that coaxing tone,
And still his eyes pronounced me fair,
 As if the world held me alone.

I scorned her then, as women can,
A creature vain and frivolous,
Whose folly had allowed this man
A sort of right to treat her thus:
John's wife! my eyes were opened wide,
For I had loved since last he smiled,
And felt why good Sir James had cried,
'How could John marry such a child!'
I had no heart to censure Fitz,
The fault was mine, and the disgrace.
I tore my bouquet into bits,
And looked my folly in the face.

I scorn myself—not him I scorn,
But left his side with footstep quick.
He cried, 'Ah, do not show a thorn,
Sweet little roses must not prick';
I sought the ball-room—he pursued,
Crying, 'O blossom fair and false,

Come back to me, my pretty prude;
  I know you'll not refuse to valse!'
His arm about my waist he slid,
  Trying to lead me to the dance.
'And if the husband *has* forbid,
  Why, we'll evade the husband's glance.'

Is this the man whose words could charm?
  While yet he tries to lead me on
I glide from his insulting arm,
  And walk across the room to John!
Touching him shyly with my hand,
  Losing the shame I can't endure,
Close to my husband's side I stand—
  I feel protected and secure!

Ah, if his noble eyes have seen,
  His noble spirit felt the scorn—
Will righteous anger come between?
  And kind protection be withdrawn?—

But while a hundred light alarms
  Whisper their little thoughts of gloom,
Sudden he clasps me in his arms
  And waltzes with me round the room!

That John could waltz I never knew,
  I'd never seen him dance at all,
As round and round we gaily flew,
  I think it an enchanting ball!—
I feel the pressure of his arm,
  My happy hair has touched his breast,
The dance has won a hidden charm;
  I could have died, I was so blest!

I felt extremely shy next day
    (Shyness is something new to me),
I thought I'd like to run away,
    And never could pour out the tea!
I blushed when we good morning said
    (And yet I tried so calm to seem),
Blushed when he handed me the bread,
    And when he asked me for the cream.

But John—alas! he was so cold,
    And on his forehead was a frown;
He was the very John of old,
    The John who snubbed and kept me down!

I grew indignant; then I felt
    No sweet permission to rebel,

Tried to forget he would not melt,
Tried to believe that all was well.

'Twas nearly ten—he was not kind—
He'd go, and never raise his eyes!
I flung discretion to the wind
(Alas, I never shall be wise!)—
'Does dancing disagree with you?'
I asked with my demurest air;
Ah, then he raised his eyes, 'tis true,
And colored to the very hair,
And in his eyes I something saw—
Something I had not learned a bit,
I could not learn it then for awe,
But think some day I'll fathom it.
'Tis gone—instead, an angry gloom,
A darkness like a thunder-cloud;
Anger, but why? at what? for whom?
I never saw him look so proud!

With sudden gesture up he rose,
His hasty steps the chamber pace,
Our glances meet, and I suppose
He read my wonder in my face.

'There is a question in your eyes,'
He said, 'in which I bear a part;
The answer in a region lies
That never can invade your heart.
There is a life you cannot live,
A joy that could for all atone,
There is a death *that* life can give,
And still that death must be my own!
I see your heart is pure and good,
I see your rectitude and strength;
Ah, had I sooner understood—
Too late the lesson's learned at length?'

Transfixed I sat—what can it be?—
When almost grasped it slips and goes;

'Ah, speak of something else!' cried he;
'That man—did he insult you, Rose?'

Softly I murmured, looking down,
'I blame myself.' 'Not him you blame?
How kind your judgment!' Did he frown?
I raised my eyes—he blushed for shame.
'Ah, pardon me!' he said, 'for that;'
He stamped—with rage I think—but why?
Turned roughly from me, seized his hat,
And slammed the door—and here am I!

John has been dreadful since that day,
Few are the words he speaks, and these
He says in such a settled way
I never can feel quite at ease!
And often, as I work or read,
Or play, or sing, my eyes I raise,
And he drops his—but that indeed
Shows that on me his eyes *did* gaze.
He has no taste for pretty girls,
He is in love with solemn books,
He told me not to cast my pearls
To swine—he does not care for looks!
Then *why* does he look at me? why?—
I think of this so ceaselessly;
I fear some day my tongue will cry,
'Ah, John, why *do* you look at me?'

He lets me drive or walk each day.
  Walking, a servant must attend;
And, driving, for a brougham he'll pay,
  Or I take airings with a friend.
He's very careful in the choice
  Of my associates. Hardly he
Allows me the least bit of voice—
  I like him to take care of me!
We go to operas and plays,
  To balls and parties, now and then,
But John's forgot his dancing days,
  He's never waltzed with me again;
And in the mornings I am good,
  I read the books he said were right—
And sometimes they are understood,
  And sometimes they confuse me quite.

I practise for two hours a day—
No march or song that fashion brings,
But with approving conscience play
Sonatas and such horrid things.
But ne'er at night he questions me
About the books, as once he would,
Or bid me play a symphony—
So where's the use of being good?

I drove to Mudie's, and I brought
  A carriage-full of steady books;
'I'll tell him about these,' I thought,
  And see how pleased my master looks:
He will not ask me what I do,
  So I'll take courage, and *converse;*
I don't talk very well, 'tis true,
  But I've known women do it worse.

'O, John!' I cried, 'my studies see—
  Science, philosophy—that's best!—
And—what's the horrid word? dear me!—
  Theology and all the rest!—
Here's "Ecce Homo"—take a look—
  A serious thing, and yet *so* light;
Colenso on the Pentateuch,
  A Bishop, John, so he's all right!

"Maurice on Future Punishment"—
 That's nice, and proves there's none, you
  know—
And "Darwin on Development"—
 That's charming, and amused me so—
And here's a poem full of force—
 Swinburne, a Cambridge man, you see,
That won't be very deep, of course,
 But surely deep enough for me!'

John looked a little pale, I thought,
 And said, his voice a little low,
'Pray, have you *read* them?'—that I ought
 He meant—I bravely answered 'No;
I've only glanced at them as yet,
 They're long, you see, and I preferred
To study them and not forget—
 I *mean* to read them, every word!'

Paper and string he slowly took,
    Tied up my books in parcel neat,
Directed them, with steady look,
    To Mr. Mudie, Oxford Street.
Then rang the bell—the man addrest,
    'Take this,' he said, in icy tone,
Drew a deep breath like one opprest,
    And cried, 'I'm glad, the poison's gone!'

But when he saw my frightened stare,
    He smiled, and all his looks unfroze,
Close to my own he drew his chair,
    And said, 'I'll choose your books, dear
        Rose!'

PART III.

THE senseless sun rose just the same,
  Proud to be bright where all is dim,
And set the Eastern sky aflame,
  And made the earth look up at him.

The selfish birds sang just as loud,
  With rapture in their roundelaye;
And in the streets the foolish crowd
  Flock as on any other day.

How could I tell that joy was not?
  That death was knocking at the door?
Or that the arrow had been shot
  To pierce *my* heart—untouched before?

Or guess whose voice will speak my doom,
  Or what the words that must be said,
When I am singing in my room,
  And they shall tell me, 'John is dead!'

'He is not dead!' I calmly said,
  And stepped into the busy street,
Only my curls upon my head,
  And little slippers on my feet.

'He is not dead!' I cried, and walked
  Where streams of eager creatures led;
And when the people stared and talked,
  I smiled, and cried, 'He is not dead!'

Men carry SOMETHING in their arms,
  Some lifeless thing that hangs about;
And mutter words like little charms,
  Reluctant to be spoken out.

They bear that Something 'neath the skies,
  And up the stairs, and to my bed;
And then I stare with helpless eyes,
  And scream, and cry, 'He is not dead!'

Men come and gather round him then,
  To grasp his wrist and feel his head,
And nod, and look at other men,
  Who nod, and answer, 'He is dead!'

They try to take me unaware,
  And make me leave him on the bed,
But still I cry—now like a prayer—
  'He is not dead! he is not dead!'

Some one who by the pillow stood
  Made bare his arm and held it so,
Till little drops of ruddy blood
  Fell trickling down so soft and slow.

A tiny stream flows by and by;
    How silent everything has grown!—
A little breath—a little sigh—
    And then a very little moan.

'Life is not quite extinct,' they said;
    'God in his mercy may restore:'
And then I shriek, 'He's dead! he's dead!'
    And stagger senseless on the floor.

I wake and cry, 'I must get up,
    John will be coming in to dine!'
Upon my lips they press a cup,
    I taste it, drink it—it is wine.
(I think they drugged the draught they gave
    To dull the anguish in my breast;
I think 'twas drawn from Lethe's wave
    To lull my breaking heart to rest.)

I wake again; the dying day
  Makes little spangles on the wall,
And as the spangles twitch away,
  I watch, but cannot think at all.

Why am I here? why have I slept?
  Why am I drest and on a bed?—
Then back the dreadful terror swept,
  Back in one moment,—John is dead!

Along the passages I creep,
  With some strange fancy shaped like this,
Suppose the dead man is asleep
  And I may wake him with a kiss.

Into the chamber where he lay
  I enter like a guilty thing;
With hushing signs they cheer my way
  And point, and make a whispering.

I trace his figure in the bed,
  With lines that do not speak of death;
But, ah, I fear his *face* is dead,
  Its ghastly whiteness stops my breath!

'He lives!' they whisper, 'and may live;'
  They let me kneel beside him there:
And then I pray, and try to give
  Some thanks, and make it *like* a pray'r.

I think my life has gone to sleep,
  And in a dream I move and act—
Why should I break my heart and weep
  For what is not a real fact?

By day and night the feeling stays,
  It is a stunned, resistless rest,
It keeps with me through nights and days,
  While still he lies in trance opprest.

Is it because his soul is laid
  In deepest trance that mine is such?
A strange *rapport* between us made
  Because I love so very much?

I know not if 'tis so or not,
  I only know 'tis like a dream—
There's nothing that I have forgot,
  And nothing like itself doth seem.

They say the child had fallen prone,
  He caught it ere the horses slid,
And took the danger for his own;
  I but reply, 'Of course he did.'

They say the child's uninjured, or
  But lightly touched; at that I stare,
And cry, 'That's what he did it for,
  Of course the child's not hurt a hair!'

And still the days and nights pass on,
  And suns and moons illume the skies,
And still I sit and watch by John,
  And still in quiet trance he lies.

Sudden, another epoch springs,
  The first has lived its life and goes,
And now he raves of many things,
  And who I am he never knows.

O wond'rous arrows (taking flight
  From aimless hands), that find a mark,
O words that are so full of light,
  Though they are spoken in the dark!

And to myself he talks of me,
  And knows not that myself am I!
His sentences set sorrows free,
  That spread their little wings and fly.

Again I saw his ghastly eyes,
O they were full of fear and pain,
As beckoning in a secret wise,
He said, 'Hush, hush—don't tell again.'

And there was something awful in
That secret air so wild and weak,
You might have sworn some dreadful sin
Lay deeper than his tongue could speak.

But all the words he ever said,
After this mystery was made,
Were, 'Can she love me now I'm dead,
Who when I lived was too afraid?'

And then he cried in wailing tone,
His poor hand making piteous sign,
Four little words—four words alone
That went straight from his heart to mine.

'She cannot love me!' that was all—
'She cannot love me!' so it ran—
My eyes let tears in rivers fall,
And still I cried, 'She can—she can!'

He loves me—I am sure of it!
And doubts my love—ah! foolish John,
Ah! foolish John, when it is writ
My eyes within—my lips upon.

How can life look a little bright,
Ere death has promised to forget?
How can my cruel heart be light,
When they may snatch him from me yet?

'I'm in Heaven, am I not?
  You are an angel with her eyes!
And you've her little dimple got,
  That used to gladden and surprise;
'Twas just before she laughed it came,
  I've often watched it dimpling in,
Yes—there it is—and quite the same.
  I'm glad you've got her pretty chin—
Poor lovely child!—she's dead, you know;
  I killed her though I loved her well,
I killed her, I ill-used her so,
  I think I'll have to go to hell.'

And then he slept—as if, alas!
  The thought of hell could soothe and bless,
And I ran peeping to the glass
  My little dimple to caress.

9

'Ah! doctor, he is calmer now,
His pulse is lower, is it not?
The lines are lighter on his brow?
I'm sure his hand is not so hot?

The doctor has a dreadful face,
Its muscles cannot move, I know,
'Tis always calm and full of grace,
And always grave—I hate it so!
And when I say that John seems eased,
And little joyful symptoms tell,
He never is more bright and pleased,
And never says that he'll get well!
If grief shall pass and I could live
A hundred years of happy space,
With every joy that life can give
I'll ne'er forget that doctor's face!

With such a question in my tone
  I asked, 'When fever's power is seen
The thoughts they speak are all their own—
  They say the very things they mean?'
He rubbed his hands and shook his head,
  And murmured (how my hate increased!)
'In fever usually is said
  The very things they mean the least!'

How many nights I sat and saw
  The sun drop lightly from the sky,
And then my heart dropped down with awe,
  Is that the way that people die?
As thought with thought became entwined
  I scarcely dared to draw my breath,
For still to my affrighted mind
  Each summer sunset seemed a death;
And yet to look I had no choice,
  So there I sat one evening bright,
When John said in a pleasant voice,
  'How red the sunset is to-night!'

A blow was stricken through my brain
  That tingled to my finger ends,

The swift delight was like a pain—
  So keenly joy with sorrow blends;
And while my every fibre shook,
  I said in tone sustained and low—
Like some one reading from a book—
  'I never saw a brighter glow.'

And then with manner calm and wise
  I held his medicine to his lips,
Looking down deep into his eyes
  To see his soul without eclipse.
And there I saw it safe and free,
  Restored to reason's lovely sway—
And that dear soul looked up at me
  With love unfathomed in its ray.

The doctor comes—I fly to him,
  And murmur words so sweet and few—
He peers above his glasses' brim,
  And nods, and says, 'Ah-ha, he'll do!'

Ah, happy moments, pause and stay,
 You surely like to be so fair—
Ah, linger too delightful day
 Whose every minute is a prayer!
Why should I live for more than this?
 Life can bestow no brighter gem,
Since on his lips I've laid a kiss,
 And stolen one away from them!
I'll hardly let him move or speak—
 I'm just as stern as I can be—
He is so very wan and weak—
 And I'm so gay and strong, you see.

Yet once he said with sad surprise
　　(So I'm not blooming, I suppose),
'Where did you get those wistful eyes,
　　And pallid cheeks, poor, pretty Rose?'

I think that life's in love with him—
  She is so eager to restore,
She will not let his eyes be dim,
  Remembering how they shone before—
She's like an artist prone to stand,
  Bewitched her fav'rite work above,
Bestowing with delighted hand
  The little charms that spring from love;
'Tis sweet to see each tender touch—
  Fresh tiny tints and sparkles bright,
While every day he gains so much,
  That every day is marked with white.

He laughs, my gay delight to see;
  Laughs at my face of cloudless bliss:

And when he laughs it seems to me,
  Heaven can have no joy like this!
And in the twilight of the day—
  The happy day that promised more—
He held my hands and said his say:
  None said so sweet a say before!

I learned how deep his love had been:
  Poor love—by folly kept at bay;
And how his heart had crowned me queen:
  Poor queen—who flung her crown away.
How wrath and love may be the same,
  And wrath be hard and love be shy;
And as I learned I blushed with shame
  At such a shallow thing as I!
Dead fell repentance, fear, and strife,
  Lost in a Heaven of delight—
To be a loved and loving wife:
  Measureless rapture—height of height!

O! John, this sick room life is sweet,
  Don't get too well as days unfold—
I can't sit smiling at your feet,
  When in your bank you count your gold!

Here comes Sir James—the door-bell rang;
  Ah, John, you are not mine alone;
I feel a little jealous pang
  That all your words are not my own.

They meet in manner somewhat proud,
  Yet hands are grasped with gesture true;
I'm glad that passing thunder-cloud
  Has left the sky of friendship blue!

John, leaning in his easy chair,
  Looks like a hero in distress—
He has a something in his air
  That thrills me with its nobleness.

I never saw a man like John,
Whose every touch can beauty make,
The ground his footstep rests upon
Is dearer for that footstep's sake.

Very tall men are worse than small—
They straggle, and are helpless quite,
Six feet is certainly too tall,
For five feet ten's the perfect height.

As for his nose, I'll never seek
To change the one ordained by fate—
Why should a nose be like a beak?
Sure Grecian statues have theirs straight.

Sir James smiles on me as he goes,
  And says, 'I think the wrong's come right,
For, though your cheek has lost its rose,
  I fancy that your heart is light.'
The glance I gave is quenched in tears,
  In happy tears that sprang and shone,
I'd not a bit of room for fears,
  I was made up of hopes alone!

He cried, 'The fight might frighten some,
  I thought that love would win the day;
Be a wise woman—stay at home
  And learn your lesson—to obey!'

He went; John's arms are round me now,
  The blissful moments speed away,

And with a kiss that seemed a vow,
He murmured, 'We will *both* obey!
For I am thine and thou art mine,
And trust is true and faith is fond.
O fairest face! O face divine!
Beloved a lover's love beyond!'

I was so full of happy care,
And so wrapped up in John, you know,
I had forgotten I was fair,
And wondered when he told me so!

www.ingramcontent.com/pod-product-compliance
Lightning Source LLC
LaVergne TN
LVHW021411110826
845150LV00007B/1883

* 9 7 8 1 4 2 5 5 1 0 9 3 0 *